Prison Days

True Diary Entries
by a Maximum Security Prison Officer

July, 2018

Introduction

It was such an amazing experience for me to release the first volume in this series. I was nervous, almost as nervous as that late Autumn day when I first stepped behind the walls. Almost. June, although to you it may have sounded like a crazy month, was a pretty average sort of month. Apart from my good friend Kon, the rest of the experiences you read about, are pretty much how most work days run here. This month, however, was not. Things happened that I would have never expected, even for this place. I am still shocked from a couple of the incidents and angry from a couple of others. I don't want to spoil the ride for you. So let's not delay any longer. Put on your seat belt, keep your arms and legs inside the moving vehicle at all times, and enjoy the ride that was July, in a maximum security prison.

I have decided to include my original introduction here as well as you may be new to the series and not read the previous month yet. For your benefit, here is my original intro.

June Introduction

I still remember the first moment I stepped into a prison. It was a cold, late Autumn evening and I was attending an information night. I had only registered my interest a couple of days prior and was surprised at the speed of the next step in the process. A process I wasn't even entirely sure I wanted to pursue. We were all screened, scanned, given a pat down and led through into a tiny room, what's known as an airlock. Once there were a number of us, around a dozen or so, an officer showed us through a door and led us down a narrow walkway, high fences on either side, topped by razor wire. To say I wasn't intimidated would b a lie. I was shitting myself. We walked through another door into a large hall, which I would later find out to be the visits centre. There were around 100 or so seats set up in the middle, of which I utilised one. No one spoke, and by the way everyone was sitting, I could tell it wasn't just me that was nervous. This was after all, maximum security.

After waiting for about twenty minutes, a tall gentleman stood in front of us, holding a microphone. He began speaking, the usual welcome, this is who I am, this is what I do kind of thing. His next sentence however, nearly changed my mind.

"It takes a very special type of person to work in Corrections." My head was already full of a complete mixture of emotions, but that sentence sounded so cliched, that I almost walked out right there. I have always been aware of sales pitches. I have worked a sales job myself in the distant past and understood the path to a sale, the steps one took to ensure a handshake at the end of the presentation. Buttering up the customer was a good beginning, and this felt like a butter up. At that moment, I felt as if this was the kind of interview where everybody was offered a role. But, for some reason I stayed. Something made me sit in that chair and wait. And now, all these years later, if I was to conduct a presentation to new prospective recruits, I believe my opening sentence would be that working in corrections takes a very special type of person. Because it really does. If you are easily offended, then don't become an officer. If you are one to run away when a fellow officer is being attacked, then don't become an officer. If the words Fuck, Shit, Cunt, Motherfucker offend you, then definitely don't become an officer. Because this world, this place behind the walls, is not what you imagine.

The first time I entered a unit housing some fifty prisoners, my heart was in my throat. We could hear the prisoners before we entered the unit, and it was loud. They were screaming so many profanities at us that for some reason, it made us all wear these goofy grins. It felt weird. It was a nervous grin for me. I remember feeling a lot of respect for the officers standing in that station, dealing with this everyday. Hindsight is funny sometimes, because I have spent many nights in that same unit,manning it by myself, alone, with the TV the only company for twelve long hours.

The officers took us to a second unit on this guided tour. It left me shocked. What I had seen on TV and what I had imagined I would see, were nothing compared to what was now before me. I had always imagined that maximum security meant maximum protection as well. For the officers. Behind thick glass and steel bars, shielded from danger. There was no bullet proof glass. There were no cages or bars or even any form of separation from the prisoners. The unit we were standing in had two floors, lines of cell doors numbering around maybe 40, running along the entire length. In the middle of the unit stood a raised platform with a step on one side that led inside. Around the platform was a circular desk with a counter top, maybe stomach height to me, with book shelves and a computer screen sitting on the desk level. Once the prisoners were released from their cells, all 60 of them, the officers would stand or sit, all three of them, in this officer's station for the duration of their shift and perform their duties. There was zero protection if anything was to go pear shaped. One of the officers taking us on this guided tour made an off the cuff remark that has stuck with me ever since. It is a remark that I have shared with new officers as well. He said

"They decide whether you go home."

I left that information session numb. I had never experienced anything like it before. I had never been in trouble with the police, nor had anything to do with prison or anyone who had been to prison. I was literally fresh. Needless to say I applied and after about three months, began my career as a Correctional Officer in a maximum security prison. The experiences I have endured since, can only be described as unbelievable. Things that happen behind these walls, never make it to the outside. It's as if the world behind the walls is on another planet. The rules change, those that exist. The rapes, stabbings, assaults, they all exist and are to be expected. But it's the other things, the day to day experiences of prisoners being prisoners and officers being officers that make you shake your head and wonder. I mean, the first time you are confronted by a prisoner who doesn't get their own way, and their decision to "bronze up" seems to be the best choice for them, that is something you think, why would you do that? Bronze up? That's a fancy term used to describe a prisoner smearing their own faeces all over themselves and their cell. Or the first time you ask a prisoner to remove a shiv that they have booted, as in shoved up their rectum. It's those experiences that made me decide to write about them. To share them with you. I really do hope you find these entries interesting because it's not the sort of thing you hear about. My place of work is hidden, almost shielded from the outside world and I would love to share just how brave my fellow officers are to turn up to work each day and endure these experiences. To risk everything. They truly are, remarkable people.

Now sit tight, hang on, and let me tell you about the day that was, in a maximum security prison.

Units

All the units in the prison are named after rivers and consist of management, step-down management, protection and main stream.

Management Units- Units that are predominately single occupancy out of necessity or punishment and have 23 hour lock ins. Prisoners only receive a one hour run out from their cell. Murray North and South are the Management Units.

Step Down Management- Units that are a step down from the 23 hour lock down. Prisoners are given extra run-outs through out the day but limited to around 3 to 4 hours. Some prisoners can mix and have joint run-outs.

Goulburn East and West are the Step-Down Management Units.

Protection Units

Yarra North and South, Loddon North and South, Glenelg East and West

Main Stream Units

Thomson East and West, Tambo East and West, Campaspe, Avoca, Maribyrnong,

Other Areas

Kitchen, Laundry, Medical Wing, The Wood Shop, The Metal Shop, The Maintenance Shop

Some Prison Terms

Air- Raiding- Yelling or abusing someone loudly in the middle of a unit.

Billet- A prisoner who is assigned a particular duty in the unit, on a daily basis, for a weekly pay packet. They hold the position until they are either transferred out, sacked or quit.

Bone Yard- A protection unit. Protection prisoners are also known as Boners.

Booted- To hide something in the anus

Boss- What prisoners call an officer. It began early last century, is a reverse insult and means "Sorry Son Of a Bitch"

Brew- A cup of Coffee or Tea

Brasco- Toilet or brasco roll is toilet paper.

Bronze Up- To cover ones' self in faeces.

Bunk- A prisoner's bed.

Canteen- A prisoner's weekly shopping or shopping items.

Cellie- A cellmate

Chook Pen- A fenced-in area attached to a unit for prisoners to walk around in. Approximately 15m by 15m depending on which unit. Management units have multiple chook pens as prisoners have individual run outs throughout the day.

Co-ee- A prisoner's co-accused

Crook- How officers refer to inmates

Dog- Someone who informs on another prisoner.

Greens or Greys- Prisoner's prison uniform.

Rock Spider- A paedophile.

Screw- How inmates refer to officers.

Shiv- home made knife or blade.

Slash Up- To self harm

The T.O.'s- Tactical Officers, that are highly trained and armed with batons and O.C. spray.

Trap- A small latch in a cell door that can be lowered to allow access. It is normally either half way up or three quarters of the way up the cell door.

Codes

Alpha- Officer needs assistance, Officer emergency

Bravo- Lock down of Unit
Charlie- Lock down of prison
Delta- Fire
Echo- Escape
Foxtrot- Fight, Prisoner on Prisoner
Mike- Medical emergency

Sunday, July 1, 2018

Called in for overtime today. Was given a choice between Visit Centre and Murray North. Murray being a management unit means prisoners are on 23 hour lock down and given an hour out in one of six chook pens. I know it can be quite challenging working in there but I decide to anyway. I haven't spent much time in there and am keen for a bit more experience.

I arrive at the unit a little after 7, around thirty minutes before my scheduled shift. Two officers are already in the unit, one the night officer, the other a 6 o'clock start. I greet both, shake hands then take my bag out the back and put my lunch in the fridge. When I come back out, the night officer gives me a brief run down of the previous night. There is one prisoner on suicide watch although only on S3 (hourly observations) and I recognise the name immediately, Jesse Thompson.
"Ah, Jesse Thompson." I say, pointing at the name. The night officer, John Simons, nods.
"Came back from hospital yesterday afternoon. He's been pretty quiet." he says, pointing at one of the monitors. Jesse is lying on his bed and appears to be sleeping. The other officer, a man named Russel Rawsley, looks at the monitor.
"Were you there when he sliced himself up?"
"Yeah, I was there. I did the cell search that sent him over the edge." I reply. Russel shakes his head.
"What a clown." Just then the door opens and two more officers enter. The full compliment of officers in Murray North is six officers by day and one by night. A supervisor is also present for most of the day. Janine Riley and Jacob Davidson wave as they walk to the back. Another officer, Paul Jackson and the Supervisor, Julia Billings, enter a few minutes later. I am asked if I want to run the book today and I agree, a little apprehensively. The book in any unit can be quite daunting, let alone a unit where I've had little experience. It involves manning the console for prisoner communications, answering phone calls and organising the running of specific events such as visits, medications and run outs. The Sup gives me a clap on the back and says

"You'll be fine, mate. Don't be shy." I smile and sit at the console. Russel and Janine grab the muster folder and make their way to the cells to begin morning count. The night officer bids us farewell and heads out, one last wave as he walks out of sight. I watch Russel and Janine as they make their way around the cells, dropping each trap and peering in. The Sup stands next to me and asks if I have heard anything about Kon. I shake my head.

"I know he is still in the coronary care unit, but not sure when he'll be let out. Probably not for a while."

"Code Black, Murray North" suddenly comes over the radio.

"What? Where?" I hear the Sup say. I look around and then up to the top tier.

"Ma'am, we need to open the cell." Janine shouts from the cell door. "He's not answering us. He's lying on the floor." The Sup walks to the stairs and I follow as Control announces the code to the prison. The Sup peers in.

"Chris. CHRIS!" She knocks on the cell door, then bangs with her fist. Nothing. She unlocks the door and the prisoner is lying on the floor, face down, his head near the door. Prisoners are known to converse with fellow prisoners by shouting under their doors, sometimes for hours depending on the topic of conversation. Lying that way could cause positional asphyxia, if left for too long in the wrong circumstances. The worst part though? There were three slices of toast lying on the prisoner's back. The night officer is supposed to provide toast to prisoners, as they have no cooking facilities in their cell, and conduct a welfare check at the same time ensuring they receive a response from the prisoner to ensure they are OK. The Sup bends down and shakes the prisoner without a response and feels for a pulse.

"No pulse." she says. She beckons for two officers to come in and then has them lift the prisoner out on to the walkway. They begin CPR immediately. I remember the unit being eerily quiet, the other prisoners not making so much as a peep. The prisoner is blue, almost purple and his eyes are partly open. The Sup leans down again and feels for a pulse, but shakes her head. The officers continue CPR until the medical team rush in shortly after and immediately take over. They begin to hook up their defib machine and one nurse asks the Sup to arrange an ambulance.

"Already on the way." she responds. The nurse nods and they continue to apply the machine. They zap the prisoner, again and again but there is no response. A doctor enters the unit and also attempts to work on the prisoner. The minutes seem to drag as the doctor and nurses desperately try to save him, hitting him again and again and again. Finally, the ambulance officers arrive and assist the nurses. They continue working for a long time, almost an hour, before they declare the prisoner deceased. He is covered in a sheet and left where he is as police are called in. He was 28 years old and a father of two.

When the police arrive, they conduct an investigation, talking to staff and taking photos, before the body is allowed to be removed. It takes another couple of hours for everything to be returned to normal and the prison is finally unlocked. In situations such as this the entire prison remains in lock down. We begin to conduct prisoner's run outs, escorting them one at a time to a designated chook pen. The mood is very solemn in the unit as we escort each prisoner out and begin our trap to trap duties.

It is nearly lunchtime count by the time everything is caught up with. The unit noise is almost back to normal, prisoners shouting to each other under the doors, the occasional burn of some "boneyard dog" somebody has an issue with. The medical trolley enters the unit and lunchtime medications are dished out trap to trap. It takes around ten minutes and as the trolley exits the unit count is called and Paul and Jacob go trap to trap and conduct muster. They show me the numbers when they finish and I call in count to control. Count is called correct 10 minutes later and we start the afternoon session. Shortly after count is called correct, the phone rings and there are visitors on the way for a prisoner. I organise for him to be brought out of his cell and into the visits box, a small cubicle we have in the unit, divided in half by a bench and thick glass. There is a small grill beneath the glass through which the people communicate with each other. The phone rings again and we have a new prisoner that needs to be picked up from the admissions building which I allocate to another 2 officers. Because every single move and escort takes 2 officers, the staff numbers can reduce quite quickly if a few things happen so I wait with some moves to ensure we don't end up short. I'd rather take my time escorting prisoners than end up with too few officers in case something kicks off.

Once the visit is finished, two officers, Russel and Jacob, head down to pick up the new arrival. Two other officers, Janine and Paul prepare the cell he will be going into. They prepare a bed pack, a TV (yes, solitary these days entitles them to a TV, and when I say "entitles" that's exactly what I mean. These prisoners know their entitlements and rather than ask for them, they demand them), and food utensils. They can bring with them food, reading material, drawing material, clothing, kettle. Nearly all the comforts of home. They return a short time later accompanying their prisoner, Ryan Blake. He is checked in, interviewed and taken to his cell. As he has been here before, more than once, Ryan knows the procedure and as such makes the process a lot simpler, not needing to run through the finer details with him. He is upbeat and chirpy as he is lead away, greeted as he walks to his cell by friends who are shouting at him from under their doors.
"Blakeeeeeyy!" one yells.
"Hey crazy cunt! Watcha doin back in this joint?" another shouts. He looks in the direction smiling, giving them a thumbs up.
"Jacks got me doin a burg." he yells back. There are several laughs from behind the doors.
"Allegations, Brother, allegations." one finishes as he enters his cell, his cuffed hands put through the trap and a bolt lowered to hold his hands in place. The door is closed and his handcuffs are removed through the trap and the bolt lifted again, the trap sealed. It never ceases to amaze me just how happy they are to come here. It takes only a few minutes before the chatter restarts, the crew welcoming their new tenant to the building.

There isn't much to report for the rest of the day. Run outs happened without incident, the afternoon medical run was completed with out too much fanfare and dinner was dished out to the prisoners, the meals rewarmed and served up door to door by the staff. The night staff member came in just before lock down muster, not the one from the previous night, we did a brief handover and walked out of the prison on time.

Monday July 2, 2018

Worked in the Visits centre today. Received news that the officer from the previous days morning events has been suspended pending an investigation. Not good. I head straight to the Visits Centre and am placed in the back again. There are 3 female officers in the front already so me and a couple of guys are only too happy to man the back and stare at penises again all day. It's a good opportunity to compare I guess.

The two officers working with me today are both fresh from the new intake and as such, quite fresh. I will have to guide them today and try and show them the ropes a bit. It can be quite confronting to have to conduct endless strip searches when still new but it does get easier quite quickly. Raj and Roger are both keen to learn and I am also happy to teach. Our shift starts after count is already correct and await our first couple of customers. The list isn't too bad today, with protection first and last and main stream in the middle. The first lot of prisoners is only 14 so we should be able to get through them relatively easy with our inexperienced team. I manage the book and enter all the prisoners coming and going into the building. I also allocate lockers and which strip room to enter. My two offsiders take a strip room each. The first four show up within a few minutes and I conduct a couple of the strips first, highlighting which parts to focus on. Once they are all processed, I speak to both Officers and highlight the importance of being extra vigilant when they return from the visits. This is one of the main areas of contraband introduction when involving visitors and we are really the last line of defence if anything does get through. They nod and acknowledge the instructions. As we wait for the next group to arrive, I share with them the syringe story from the last time I was in here and the laughing lasts until the next group enter the door (see June Edition). 3 more prisoners enter with their escort officer and I enter them in the book, directing two to their respective strips. The third, a prisoner called Cooper Taylor stands quietly, waiting for his turn. I ask him if he is excited about his visit and he tells me that he can't wait to see his partner and little girl. She is 1 next week and I see the sadness in his eyes when he tells me he wont see her for her birthday. I tell him that she is probably a very good reason to try and stay out of prison and he nods. Raj beckons him over as his prisoner heads inside.

The prisoners continue to come in sporadically over then next hour. I call the two officers over and remind them of the importance of being really thorough with the strips once they start coming back out. I highlight the fact they can hide things in their mouths, butts and eye of their penises, between their toes, anywhere. Eventually the first ones start coming back out and they take two straight in and conduct their strips. I can make them out through the doorway and see they are taking their time which is good. The last group of prisoners come in for their visits and we have a bit of a cross over. A couple start arcing up but we quickly settle them down and continue to process. As each prisoner is finished with their finishing strip, I contact their units for their escort who enter soon after. The day is running pretty smoothly and it feels like a well oiled machine for three blow ins who don't normally work in here. I see Cooper coming back out, a smile missing from his face. He is looking quite stern, not angry just serious, or nervous. Roger calls him over and conducts the strip. I spot for him and don't notice anything out of the ordinary. I ask him how his visit went and he said it went good, loved seeing his baby girl, a smile appearing but quickly fading again. I call for his escort back to Yarra North and they are there within a few minutes. I decide to give the unit a call and just let the officers know that even though his visit went well he seemed nervous about something. Maybe nothing but it doesn't hurt to give a heads up. They thank me and hang up.

We process each prisoner as they come back out from their visit and pretty soon its another waiting game waiting for the main stream. It doesn't take long and before we know it, we have a room full of ins and a few outs all waiting to be processed. A couple of them try to burn the new officers but we quickly process them and move them on. It's a game to them and they know exactly how to play it. Especially when they have finished what they came for and it's 5 minutes before count and being processed is the difference between making it back to the unit to eat lunch or being stuck here for lunchtime muster. So they manipulate the system by "playing the game". Make an officer uncomfortable and he will process you next to get you out of there. Unless of course it's an officer with some experience behind him who will go the opposite and make them last in line instead. Like I said, it's a game.

Lunchtime muster is called a short time later and thankfully we have managed to process all the prisoners who had finished. We walk around the building counting our numbers, including the front, and give the desk staff our numbers. They call it in and five minutes later its called correct and the afternoon begin. Ten minutes or so pass and more prisoners enter for their visits while others have completed theirs. The game starts again for the second half.

The afternoon runs just as the morning did and we are processing them in a steady stream. Main streamers are soon all finished and gone and protection are ready to begin their afternoon run. Things are flowing just like we were hoping. It's around 4 o'clock when there is a code called on the radio.
"Code Mike Yarra North." is the call. I check the sheet and there are no prisoners due from that unit for visits as they all pretty much had the morning stretch. We continue to process the ones we have and then wait for the code to be stood down. A minute or so later a second call comes across the radio and it is the sort of call that brings shudders. Not because of what it is, but because you can actually hear the panic and anguish in the officer's voice. "Yarra North! I need urgent medical help in Yarra North!!" As we still have a number of prisoners waiting to be stripped and a couple now coming out, none of us are able to go and assist the unit. Another minute passes and we hear radio chatter begin about an ambulance being on its way, gates to be manned and ready for them and staff readying themselves to go on the escort to the hospital. We see a number of staff come running past the door where we are and it doesn't look good. No new prisoners will be

escorted to the visits area while the code is in progress so all we can do is wait once we have finished processing everyone. I see one of my mates come walking past the door and I crack it and ask him whats happening.

"Crook just died in Yarra North. OD." he says. I close the door.

"Fuck, two in two days." I think to myself. Another twenty minutes pass and a Sup comes in through the door. It's Bruce and he has a very serious look on his face. I ask him if everything is OK and he shakes his head.

"Think he swallowed a balloon." He doesn't need to tell me who the prisoner is. I have already guessed and in time am proven correct. Cooper Taylor. I shake my head, but am not surprised. Unfortunately this is prison and he could have swallowed that balloon for any number of reasons. From being threatened or forced to money or favours. I know there is one child that isn't going to care why. She just lost her Dad.

The prison is locked down for the rest of the day. Ambulance and Police officers remain in the prison for a couple more hours and we have already gone home by the time everything is cleared. I find out from a friend later in the evening what happened as far as they could tell. Cooper's visitor had been strip searched when she came into the prison but nothing was found. They think she hid the balloon in her vagina. Video footage rules out the balloon being in the nappy as neither mum nor dad ever reach in throughout the visit. Taking an infant, or any visitor for that matter, to the bathroom, instantly converts the visit to a boxed one, meaning no contact and that didn't happen. They do see mum reach into her pocket quite deep and move her hand around, suspecting she had ripped a hole in her pocket so she could reach in and pull it out. There was a packet of chips on the table between them and she had simply pulled the balloon out, reached for a chip, leaving the balloon in the packet and then Cooper went in for a handful, including the balloon, and simply put the lot in his mouth and swallowed, together with a swig from the orange juice they had. It was also described to me that as the officers were conducting CPR on him, Cooper began leaking thick reddish brown fluid from his mouth and nose. The term he used was "he looked like a frozen coke machine." I felt sick. But more so I felt sad. Not for Cooper. Prisoners make their own choices everyday and I have no sympathy especially when drugs are involved. But I do feel sad for his daughter.

Tuesday, July 3, 2018

Am rostered in Visits again to day and find a familiar face as I enter the unit. Clare's smiling face greets me and I welcome her back after her hot watering incident last month (see June Edition). "Welcome back stranger. How you feeling?" I ask her. "Good. Glad to be back." she responds. "You our sup today?". She nods at this and I am happy to see her back again. I am working with the same crew as yesterday and that is a good thing. They did well and I was glad to be with officers that were as keen as them.

I check the list and see it will be quite a busy day. It is an entire day of main stream and that means prisoners will be coming and going without escorts all day. Raj and Roger enter a few minutes later, we shake hands and they put their bags away. They are keen to discuss the death from the previous day and I fill them in on what I know. I also reassure them that there is nothing they could have done. We aren't allowed to perform internal searches, with prisoners or visitors. As sad as it is, what happened was of their own doing. We leave it at that and just as the two put gloves on, the door buzzes and I buzz four prisoners in, starting another day of strips.

Two prisoner take seats and two are taken into separate strip rooms, as Raj and Roger begin the first round. I can hear one of the prisoners ark up, annoyed at how slow the process is taking and Raj calming him down. I go and stand just behind Raj, making myself visible. Sometimes just having another officer present is enough to stop a situation from escalating. It works on this occasion and once finished, he heads inside. Sometimes complaining over an extra thirty seconds is not worth risking your visit over. The door buzzes and another five prisoners are let in while Raj and Roger finish the first group. One of the new ones is a prisoner called Tully Johnson. He is renowned for baiting officers and at 6 foot 6, can be quite intimidating. His favourite target? New officers. He sits, already grinning as he checks out the two newbies working with me. He looks at me and waves.

"Hi Boss." he says, grinning widely.

"Hello Tully." I respond. Roger beckons him over and his grin broadens, gets up and goes in the strip room. I can hear him starting almost immediately, his voice loud and obnoxious. I stand just behind Roger but Tully knows out tricks and doesn't let go. He is currently discussing the prettiness of Roger's man bun. Asking him if he's had it long and what his boyfriend thought of it. I am not surprised when Roger begins going faster. I ensure he still performs all the right checks and we move him on, the other prisoners laughing as he walks past. We finish the rest after a few minutes and enjoy a small break, the place empty. We expect another 22, staggered between now and lunchtime, some three hours away. A code Mike is called for one of the far units and we can breathe easy as no prisoner movements occur during a code. I walk in the front and see how the visits are going.

Three female officers are manning the front and wave at me as I walk into the station. Julie, Rachel and Emily are all experienced officers, the least having 4 years. They have several monitors in front of them, cameras scattered around the large room. A children's section is off to one side and there are a couple playing there now. I see one of the cameras is trained on Tully, who is being visited by a blonde lady, wearing tight jeans and a tight t shirt and a jacket that hung open around her. I leave the ladies to it and head back to the strip area. The code is stood down a few minutes later and the buzzer goes off a few minutes after. Another three prisoners enter as two from the front also return. We begin processing each and sending them on their merry way.

We are about to send the last of them out when I hear yelling from the front followed by a code alpha in visits. Raj ushers the last prisoner out as Roger and I bolt to the front, the yelling now louder. As we reach the Visits hall we see Emily and Rachel standing near Tully, that wide Cheshire grin beaming. He is holding something and it looks like he spilled something down the front of his shirt. His girlfriend is also standing and has the same thing over her face. As we get closer, we see the issue. And its pretty straight forward. What he is holding is his dick. What he has spilled is semen, across his girlfriend's face and on his t shirt. He begins putting his dick back in his pants as other prisoners begin howling and cheering. A mum has gone over to her children in the play area and is shielding them. Tactical Officers burst in and begin escorting Tully out of the area, that Cheshire grin never wavering. His girlfriend is also grinning' although she is cleaning herself up, wiping semen from her face, although she isn't wiping it on any tissue or towel. That, she busily licks from her fingers, giggling. Tully will face charges, although to him, serving 14 years for armed robbery, the 10 second blowjob he received, will be totally worth the loss of TV for a week.

The scene is quickly brought under control and within a few minutes the visits area is back to normal. The dozen or so prisoners still seeing their visitors have calmed again and within an hour, all the prisoners have been rotated out, new ones taking their places.

Lunchtime muster comes and goes with out incident and we continue to process prisoners through out the afternoon. Around 2 o'clock a Code Alpha is called for one of the back units. We have half a dozen prisoners currently being processed and are unable to attend, although we see quite a few officers go rushing past our door. The call was from a female officer and her panic was clearly conveyed through her voice. A few minutes pass and a second call is put out, requesting all available officers. It lets the prison know that its more serious than just a simple confrontation. We only have a couple of prisoners left and Raj runs out the door to assist. Roger and I continue with our duties, finishing the last two together. When the prisoners are through to the hall, we follow and see the girls talking. We head over and they tell us that three officers have been assaulted in Tambo West, one quite bad. Jeff Stebbins was knocked out cold and another had a broken jaw. The female officer had managed to call a code but was also attacked, we didn't know how bad yet. This was definitely not a good start to the month and we still had almost 4 weeks to go. I was about to ask Roger if he wanted to run down, when another call came across the air, a code Charlie. Roger looked at me puzzled and I mouthed "Lock Down" to him. The entire prison was about to be locked down. That would mean resources were stretched to breaking point and if something kicked off now, they would struggle to respond.

"Sorry everyone, we have to lock down the prison. Visits unfortunately are cancelled for the time being." Emily calls out and we hear a group sigh reverberate around the centre, some swearing and one prisoner begin to argue. But Emily holds her own and shuts any argument down.
"You heard the code, guys. We have to lock down." I am thankful that the prisoners in the centre don't include trouble makers. It appears that most of them are fairly new, and the two only long termers are both in their sixties and mostly beyond confrontation. We shuffle all the prisoners to the back and begin to process them, most clearly not happy. But unfortunately our hands were tied and they seemed to understand. A couple of officers had been allocated to help us return the crooks back to their respective units and the visits centre is cleared out by the time we return from our first drop off.

The code stays in place for the rest of the day and the prison remains in lock down. All up, there were four officers hurt, three requiring medical attention, five prisoners hurt with four needing medical attention. The unit also had OC spray deployed and would need to be decontaminated. A number of staff were overcome by the effects and also took the rest of the day off. There were several ambulances deployed to ferry the injured to hospital and extra officers deployed to assist with all the moves. The five prisoners who attacked staff were all quickly isolated and removed from the prison entirely, being immediately transported to another nearby maximum security facility.

Both Roger and I are redeployed to help with afternoon moves, medical rounds and meals. We each escort a medical trolley to a unit and conduct medical rounds trap to trap. It's a long process but just how it is during a lock down.

My legs are well and truly aware of the walking they do for the final few hours and I am glad once the final muster is finished.

Today was not a good day.

Wednesday, July 4, 2018

Rostered Off

Thursday, July 5, 2018

Rostered Off

Friday, July 6, 2018

Rostered Off.

Saturday, July 7, 2108

Called in for overtime. Worked as a General Duties Officer and thus had several duties throughout the day. The prison has returned to normal after the drama from previous days. I check my emails as soon as I get in and read up about all those injured and all are doing well. All have left hospital except for one and he is doing OK and in very good spirits. I run into Supervisor Bruce Stephens while walking to my first duty and he whispers that Shane Roberts had been suspended pending an investigation into the rapes of the two boys the previous month (see June Edition). I shake my head. Why would anyone want to throw away a twenty year career for the sake of plain bad attitude and laziness? We shake hands and part ways, him to his unit, me to the medical wing to escort a medical trolley to a unit for morning medications once count is called correct.

I escort the nurse and her trolley to Tambo East and as we enter the unit there is silence. A couple of crooks are milling around the toasters and one is on the exercise bike in the far corner. A few are sitting around a couple of tables eating breakfast but other than a couple whispering to each other, the unit is quiet. The nurse wheel s the trolley into her dispensing room and I give the officers in the station the thumbs up to call the prisoners down for morning medication. They comply and within a couple of minutes there is a neat line outside the door. It feels eerie to have no noise and it's almost unsettling. It almost feels like something is in the air but I try not to let it bug me too much. Each prisoner comes in, shows their ID card and then present their open mouth to me for inspection after downing their pills. One prisoner has forgotten his ID card but rather than firing up, simply walks back to his cell and gets it, returning a short time later. He goes through the motions of getting his meds and all prisoners are finished shortly after. I look at the officers in the station and hold my hands up in a "what's going on" gesture and they shrug their shoulders in a "Don't know" reply. I wave bye to them and the nurse and I head next door to Tambo West.

Chalk and cheese is the only way I can describe the transition from one unit to the other and the units are practically next door to each other. We can hear the shouting even before we open the doors and the nurse looks at me, grinning.

"Wow." is all I can manage. She enters her dispensing room and I enter the unit to find two prisoners yelling at each other on the top tier from within each of their cell doors. It appears that one had been offered a single cell on the bottom tier and the other believed he was more entitled to it. Single cells are a valued commodity. You could sleep in peace, shit in peace, masturbate in peace without constantly having to hide or keep quiet or hold your shit in for 10 hours because you simply didn't need to go during unlock. When a prisoner transfers into a unit, their name is added to the bottom of the "single cell" list and once your name reaches the top, you are offered the next available single cell when a prisoner transfers out. Sometimes the wait can be months and so things can get quite heated when someone believes they are entitled to one more than someone else. In this case, prisoner Wiebeck believed he had a claim to cell 11 over prisoner Earnshaw. One officer, Tom Barkley, was standing next to Earnshaw, red, flustered and unsure of what to do. Another officer, Mike Renshaw, was yelling for Wiebeck to shut the hell up and come down to the station before he called a code. The third officer, Amy Smith, waved at me and called for morning medications. Renshaw ended up going up to the top tier and locked Wiebeck down until he calmed down. Wiebeck followed all instruction so as not to cop a disciplinary charge and quietened down once the cell door was locked. Earnshaw wanted to continue and was told to let it go and move his shit to the new cell.

A couple of the prisoners decided they wanted different doses to what the doctor had prescribed and were voicing their dismay at the nurse for not doing as they said. Funny that. They will try though. The nurse held her own and put them back in their place, telling them to make another appointment with the doctor. They gave up and complied with her requests, taking their meds and presenting to me. Another prisoner, Fraser, took his pills, turned to me and quickly walked off, but I had seen the flash of red capsule, calling him back to show me his mouth a second time. He did and the capsule was gone. Again, funny that.

When we finish our allocation of units, I escort the nurse back to the medical wing and bid her farewell. I next have gate duty in the quadrangle for an hour. There are a number of gates that have adjoining building and corridors, all needing access to protection and main streamers alike. As they couldn't mix, we had to act as traffic lights, halting some gates while releasing others. Main streamers loved hanging out at their gates while protection prisoners filed past, giving them everything they had. It would be scary to think of what could happen if we allowed them in. Or if someone screwed up and mixed them.

I man the gates for an hour, monitoring my radio for movement requests and allocating gates to open and close as needed, each one opened by hand with a key. Two other officers help and open gates as I allocate them. We take it in turns with who opens and closes gates and who monitors the radio and in a very short time, the hour is up. It's all fun and games.

Once I finish the gates, I have a spare hour before lunchtime count and I go to Visits and see if they need a hand. The Duty Sup will radio if he needs me, his daily work sheet highlighting when officers are available. I enter the unit just as a code mike is called in Tambo West. As I am on general duties and in between jobs, I head over to see if I can lend a hand. As I enter the unit, I see officers standing at a cell door on the bottom tier, cell 11. I begin to help another officer lock down prisoners. Code mikes are normally just medical and don't require units to be locked down, but another officer asks me to help and I comply. I find out after that shortly after the nurse and I had left the unit, Earnshaw had moved all his belongings down to his new cell and Wiebeck was compliant and was allowed out of his cell. The officers had seen Wiebeck shake Earnshaw's hand then proceed to jump on the exercise bike for an hour. Without making it obvious, Wiebeck had jumped off the bike at some point and entered Earnshaw's new cell. He was quite a bit bigger than Earnshaw and probably scared the smaller prisoner into submission. He had simply snapped the interior lock in place, grabbed the smaller prisoner, then forced him onto the bed, raping him repeatedly for around thirty minutes. The Tactical boys already had Wiebeck and were walking him out of his cell and down the stairs. Earnshaw was lying face down on his bed, blood on his buttocks and the bed linen. A nurse was inspecting his butt and the duty sup was on the phone, probably calling an ambulance.

A stretcher is wheeled into the unit and Earnshaw hobbles onto it, face down. A couple of prisoners start hooting, obviously more on Team Wiebeck than Team Earnshaw, but one look from an officer and they call it off. The stretcher is wheeled out a short time later and eventually Earnshaw is taken to hospital. He returned later that night and was taken back to his cell.

Lunchtime count is called shortly after and I stay in the unit to help out with muster and subsequent lunch through traps. The cell is a crime scene and Intel staff inspect it before anything else. The unit is eventually unlocked and it goes back to normal quite quickly. I leave to meet the nurse and commence afternoon meds.

We head to Campaspe unit first and as we enter the unit, I see one officer on the top tier, doing a security walk. Another officer is sitting in the station and the third is in the office. The station officer sees me and beckons me over. I don't know them. I walk over and introduce myself, finding out he is from the new course, Frank Turner. He asks me to go and see the officer in the office as she doesn't seem to be quite right.

I walk to the office and walk in, the smell of alcohol quite strong. The officer is sitting at the desk and smiles when she sees me. It's Thelma. Hey eyes are bloodshot and she is eating a bowl of grapes.
"Everything OK, Thelma?" I ask her.
"All good mate." she replies, but her voice is garbled , her eyes opening and closing in a tired, worn out parody.

"Grape?" she offers, holding up the bowl. I oblige and take one, popping it in my mouth. I sit and am about to ask her if she needs help, when the taste of vodka fills my mouth. Its strong and bitter taste instantly overtaking my mouth. I spit the grape out in my hand and am about to ask her something when the duty sup enters. He takes one look and asks me to escort her back to his office. She goes to grab her grapes but he takes them first. She gives him a disgusted look but follows me out of the office and out of the unit. A couple of prisoners start laughing as we walk past and mutter something unintelligible. Thelma is half staggering as she hangs on to my arm. We don't speak and I take her to the duty sup's office and sit with her. Eventually we get a call from the duty sup to say Thelma's husband is waiting out the front of the prison and she is escorted out.

It turns out, Thelma had been injecting vodka into her grapes and was smuggling them in through the front in her lunch box. No one had ever checked them and she had been able to sneak them in for God knows how long. She is suspended pending an investigation. Thelma's special grapes will probably turn into an urban legend eventually. Hopefully she doesn't lose her job completely. Although I don't like her chances for keeping it.

Another officer had finished my afternoon medical run and I complete my afternoon by returning to Campaspe where they are now an officer short. The other two are busy chatting when I come back in and both begin questioning me when I enter the station. Having an officer drunk on duty is not an every day occurrence and before long, the phone begins to ring with inquisitive questions. We spend the afternoon answering a multitude of questions over the phone and have multiple visitors drop in.

It's just as well that the afternoon goes by incident free and the prisoners leave us to our own devices. I end up applying for some annual leave for the end of month for a week beginning Saturday the 28th. It ended up being a strange day considering all that happened and as I drive home that night I think about what would make an officer feel so depressed that they would consider smuggling alcohol into a prison to then get pissed on the job, not only endangering yourself but the officers around you.

Sunday, July 8, 2018

Today I was rostered in Reception. It is located at the front of the prison and is outside the walls hence no prisoner contact. There are six officers working in this area in the front area and one x-ray officer who sits behind a partition and runs all bags and personal items through an x-ray machine. The security measures in place to ensure there is no contraband smuggled in to the prison include random pat downs, random strip searches, a metal detector called a wand waved over each person, contraband detection dog, x-ray machine and random drug swabs. I am assigned to the x-ray machine and being a Saturday know that the day will be a massive one. It is one of the biggest visitor days and most sessions in the visits centre are booked out solid. I begin my shift at 7am, just in time to check the bulk of the day staff coming on for their shift and it's a non stop process for a solid hour.

Once count is correct we beckon visitors to come in and we begin processing each one. There are Mums, Dads, sons, daughters, friends and whole families. Some are friendly while some are not so friendly. Others can be downright painful. Especially like one Mum who we weren't processing quick enough.
"Can you hurry up? Here to see my fuckin son." she barks at the crew at the desk. It's always so much easier when they swear as you normally use that as the first line of defence.
"Please don't swear at me. You won't miss out." Samantha responds to the lady calmly and you just know she gets even more wound up. She waves at her to come forward and the detection dog gives her a once over. Samantha then takes a swab of her purse, running the detector tab along all sides, as well as her hands. Another officer, James, gives the lady a pat down and asks her to turn her pockets inside out which she does, frowning and mumbling under her breath. Samantha comes back a couple of minutes later and informs the lady that her swab returned a positive reading for Cocaine and her visit would be switched to a boxed visit. She begins to holler and complain, her voice get louder and louder but she knows it's no use. If she causes too much of a scene then her visit will be cancelled altogether and she

gives in, again mumbling under her breath. She is led through to a holding room with another group and eventually escorted to the visits area.

The day is long and doesn't let up. I run the x-ray machine for the bulk of the day only taking a break for lunch and a short stint running the wand for an hour. There really isn't much to say about today. It's just a busy day of processing visitors without any flare ups or incidents. We hear a couple of code mikes in the prison but they are normal run of the mill codes with nothing really to report. One was a bit bizarre where a prisoner was doing push ups with his feet up on a chair. He apparently was trying to impress his mates and was clapping his hands in between each push up and ended up falling down flat on his face, two teeth snapped on the concrete floor and cutting his lip quite badly.

Other than that it was a run of the mill day and I'd rather not bore you with filling each page with meaningless words that wont hold your interest.

Monday, July 9, 2018

Rostered Off

Tuesday, July 10, 2018

Rostered Off

Wednesday, July 11, 2018

 Today I was called in for overtime and choose Visits again. I enjoy working in here, especially if I am out the back. It's like a little hidden world, away from the outside. It's just a place to do your processes and go home. Raj is with me again and I greet him as I walk in. Russel Rawsley is there as well and we shake hands. "You are going to love today, Mr. King, Sir." Raj says to me, beaming a moon smile at me.
"Why?" I ask. He holds a sheet of paper out to me. My smile grows as I inspect it. All the visits for that day fill less than half the page. 14 in total.
"What?" I say, but my smile remains intact. Vanessa Green walks in from the front.
"Morning Gents. How do you like the list for the day?"
"Is this for real?" I ask her and she nods. I fist pump the air.
"Now that is the sort of OT I like." I add.
"That list and OT? Lucky fuck." Russel says disgusted but he is joking, slapping me on the back as he walks passed me.
"Why so small?" I ask of Vanessa and she shrugs her shoulders. I don't complain and put my bag away. We have 6 prisoners between now and lunch and then 8 for the afternoon, the last booked in for 4.30. I find out later that the visits booking system malfunctioned and all visits were scrubbed, only able to be re-booked the day before. There wasn't enough time to fill the schedule so we have been given a gift and no-one complains.

The first couple of prisoners enter soon after and Raj and I process them while Russel mans the book. I strip my prisoner, inspect his clothing, check him and allow him to redress himself. He heads inside almost skipping. Raj finished his as another two prisoners enter. I repeat the process and within five minutes we are two thirds through our morning work load. I follow the prisoner through the door and go and sit in the officers station in the visits hall, greeting the officers there. Vanessa is monitoring the screens and judging by the quietness of the room, doubt whether she needs to focus too hard. There are only four prisoners and only one has more than one visitor.

We talk shit for an hour or so, even giving the prisoners a little extra time. The others ask me about Thelma and I tell them what I know. It's a sad story and we don't dwell on it too long. After giving the prisoners and extra twenty or so minutes we take them back and reprocess them back in. They all check out clean and as we send them out, our last two for the morning come in. They are processed and in to their visitors in a few minutes. Lunchtime muster occurs during their visit and again we give them extra time. Once their time is up we usher them back to the strip rooms and they are all jovial, happy to have been given extra time. They are finished and leave the building as we wait for the afternoon rush to come.

The afternoon is even better than the morning. The prisoners come in dribs and drabs and we process each as they arrive. It's almost one at a time for most of the afternoon and only once do we have two at once. Once the last is processed and out the door, we sit around again and talk shit for a while. We all know that some days in here can be trying, busy and quite confronting when crooks or visitors get pissed off, but today is definitely not one of those days.

I drive home later that evening whistling, happy to have a fatter paycheck and happy that the day went so well.

Today was a good day.

Thursday, July 12, 2018

Today I was rostered in Admissions. I know just what to expect as I make my way there, knowing I will be staring at penises again all day. It's a funny place to work with some of the humour thrown around certainly not fit for human consumption. If the things said inside prison were spoken out in the real world, you could bet that people would find themselves out on their ear in no time. For some reason, things are just accepted in prison though.

I go and see the officer that has the day's run sheet and see that the day is pretty average. There are around 20 courts for the morning and then around the same transferring out of the prison after muster. The afternoon has around a dozen or so prisoners transferring in to the prison. Compared to some days, it can be seen as a fairly easy day. This week was starting to look like a cruise in the park, although nowhere near as easy as the week between Christmas and New Year when the transfers and courts come to an almost stand still.

We begin processing courts almost immediately, stripping each one and placing them into a holding cell. Its a little after 6 and everyone is still sleepy, so no one is really thinking about firing up. The process doesn't take too long and before the sun is even rising, we are helping to load the prisoners on to their respective buses. Once all the prisoners are all loaded, we have breakfast.

Count is called and as we are empty, it's just a simple waiting game for us until it's called correct. Once it is, we wait for our transfers to make their way up to admissions and we begin the task of processing them out. They bring all their property from their cell up with them and we have the rest of their property stored in a tub. Once they are up here, it's just a simple process of marking off a checklist to ensure they still have everything they took to their cell or deleting what they have disposed of. It's also the perfect time to see just who has been helping themselves to other people's property via stand-overs or theft. There are usually a couple per day and today is no different. One crook in particular has four different pairs of runners, 3 Nike and 1 Asics, yet there are only a single pair of prison issue runners on his property sheet. After quite a bit of arguing back and forth, he finally gives in and surrenders 3 pairs, being allowed to keep 1. Of course he chooses the most expensive looking Nikes.

All the transfers are eventually processed and sitting in their cells waiting for their buses, again, each heading in a different direction. They start to get restless around 11 o'clock and begin banging on their cell doors. Some of the officers do the rounds, letting them know that the buses shouldn't be too far away, but we don't know how long they will be and pretty soon the building is echoing to the sounds of cell door bashing. The clanging reverberates through the corridors makes conversation difficult. Fortunately for us, it's not our first day and we know how to sweet talk them, bribing them into silence. Lunch. We simply start to hand out sandwiches to the prisoners and pretty soon admissions is sweetly quiet, like a day care centre during afternoon nap.

Shortly after, the buses begin rolling in and we load each as they show up. Within half an hour, we are empty again, all transfers now out for their road trips. Lunchtime muster is called shortly after and again we pull the lucky straw, being empty of prisoners. It is called incorrect some 20 minutes later and we wait as the prison conducts a recount. It is finally called correct 45 minutes late. Immediately upon correct, buses begin to roll in with some of our afternoon transfers. There are 4 from one jail and 2 from another. There is also a third bus with a couple of court returns. Once the paperwork is all checked out, we begin taking them off the buses and putting them into individual cells until they can be properly inducted. The court returns are taken around to the strip rooms and processed back into the jail. I take one and another officer takes another. I begin the stripping process, then hear the officer next to me begin his. He is fairly new but has never worked in admissions before. He has a spotter just like me but he is being allowed to run it his way.
"OK, lets strip down to your birthday suit and hand me your

clothing." he begins. The prisoner must have been having a bad day because he begins heckling the officer instead.

"Want me to strip you homo fuck? Like this?" he says as he strips his pants and jumper, tossing each item to the officer who in turn passes it behind him to his spotter for inspection. "Like what you see, faggoty freak?". The officer doesn't speak, but continues with the strip. The prisoner is naked now and grabs his dick, twirling it around in a circle.

"Could you stop masturbating and let me conduct this strip search?" he finally says and the prisoner   starts yelling more abuse.

"I bet you'd love me to masturbate for you. Love what you see?" he says and the officer fires back just as fast.

"I'm sorry, I don't have my glasses on, I cant see it." He then beckons for the prisoner to present his fingers, hands, open mouth, arm pits, penis, butt and feet for inspection and completes the process. When the prisoners are gone, I pat him on the back and congratulate him for keeping his cool. He did well under the circumstances and he thanks me for the compliment.

All of a sudden there is a commotion coming from one of the main cells where there are four prisoners held. One of the officers lowers the trap and peers inside, immediately withdrawing, holding his nose.

"Boss, he shit himself." comes through the trap and upon looking inside, I see three prisoners holding their noses, almost climbing the wall. I crack the door and wave them out, placing them in the cell next door. The stench is unbelievably strong, the fourth prisoner deciding he wanted to let rip in his pants. He simply sat on the bench watching as the others filed out, not embarrassed in the least. I close the door again and am glad not to be a regular. They would need to take him out, have him wash and change and then interview him. Another bus arrives and it is more courts. We take them off and into the building, filing past shit pants, and take them to the strip rooms. They are all processed and returned to their units within a few minutes. Shit pants is escorted through to a holding cell with a shower and given a new set of clothes, the soiled ones bagged in a haz-mat bag. Once he is finished, he is also processed and soon in his new unit.

The rest of the day is a similar process and no events worth mentioning. There are a couple of code mikes called, but that's about it.
Today was a good day.

Friday, July 13, 2018

Today I was rostered as a Urinalysis Officer. In laymen terms, I was going to be conducting piss tests all day. But today was Friday the 13th and of course nothing was going to be as simple as that. There were two teams of piss testers and each team consisted off three officers. One who would be manning the booth and contacting units to send prisoners up, the other two actually conducting the tests. My offsider? Tony Malone (see June Edition). I literally groaned inside when I saw him. All I could ask myself was who had I pissed off to deserve this. But I knew there was nothing I could do, so I shook hands with him and the other officer and we checked our list. We had 30 names on it and planned our strategy for the day. Who we would start with, which units and where we would end. Once we had finished, Tony and I entered the test room and the third officer went into the booth and began contacting units. We ensured we had all the equipment in good supply and ensured we wouldn't run out of anything.

The first prisoner arrives and we take him into the test room. Our first job is to strip him and ensure he doesn't have anything on him to adulterate the sample. Or possess a clean sample which to substitute for his own. Prisoners have many varied and ingenious ways with which to mess with the urinalysis process. The most common is to cut the finger off a rubber glove and have a clean prisoner piss into it. They then tie it off and somehow hide it on their person, the methods of which are numerous. It takes a very alert officer to pick up a fake sample. But it does happen quite frequently so we remain vigilant. I start the stripping process and Tony takes care of bagging the sample once we have it.

The room is set up in such a way that the officers have a perfect view of the prisoner no matter which way he turns. There is a toilet in the far corner and a convex mirror hanging on the wall above. When the prisoner turns to urinate, we can still keep an eye on what they are doing. The prisoner strips for me and I inspect every piece of clothing he has. I then inspect him from a distance, paying particular attention to his anus, underside of his penis and foreskin, common hiding places. They all check out and he gets dressed again. He grabs a jar and urinates into it. Once he finishes, Tony seals and labels the jar then seals and labels a sample bag. The prisoner signs each process and once completed is allowed to return to his unit. When we let him out, there are already 3 prisoners waiting in holding cells. We ask each if they are ready to piss and one of them is. We lead him into the room and repeat the process, paying particular attention to his underwear and pockets of his track-pants. They all check out and he takes a jar and immediately begins to urinate. We repeat the process once he is finished and when he leaves the test room we are down to 28 to finish. We do our rounds of the holding cells and another one is happy to have a go. We lead him into he room and he seems a little too keen to begin. My senses are instantly peaked when he is smiling and laughing about having to do a piss test. But his strip checks out fine and he produces as asked. Nothing out of the ordinary. We finish bagging and tagging his sample and lead him out of the room. As he passes the holding cells "All good, Boys" to the prisoners in the cells and walks out. Now I know something is up. I ask Tony if his sample was warm and he nods.

"Think he got one by us?" he asks.

"I know he got one by us." I reply. "Just don't know how." I add. We knock on a couple more cells and another prisoner is given the go ahead to produce. I switch positions with Tony this time to try and see a different point of view. The prisoner again is all smiles and complies with Tony's requests. I can sense something is odd but am unsure of what. He takes a jar and turns toward the toilet, shielding himself from our eyes. We can see the mirror but can't quite make out his hands and penis. I can see that he is fiddling a bit and sneak over while he is concentrating and looking down. I peer around his body and cringe. Sticking out of the end of his dick are three straws, each with a tiny eraser you find at the end of pencils, jammed into the end.

"I'll take those." I say and the prisoner just about jumps into the toilet bowl, completely unaware that I was there. He was trying to unplug the straws and hadn't heard me. He pulls all three straws out and tries to throw them in the toilet but I grab his arm and

Tony grabs the straws. We are gloved up, by the way. He surrenders and gives up, the smile finally leaving his face. "How the hell did you jam them down there?" I ask but he isn't talking. We lead him back to a holding cell and inform him he will be waiting for the Sup.

"Nice job." I say to Tony and he smiles back. We bag the straws, each one cut down to around 4 inches and it looks like they are melted closed at one end. Together, the 3 straws held just enough urine for the sample to be sufficient. As we bag the evidence, I wonder how many more of the prisoners had hidden samples shoved down their piss holes. I cringe again.

We ask the cells again and another prisoner volunteers. He is morbidly obese and is out of breath after walking the 20 or so steps from the holding cell to the piss room. I can see as soon as he turns to piss that he isn't hiding any straws in his penis. For one, it is almost completely hidden and only about an inch visible. The other reason? He can not reach it. He struggles to reach it with one hand while trying to twist as hard as he can but it is almost near impossible. He exhales loudly and manages to just grip the head, grunting and groaning while trying to keep a hold of it. He farts loudly from the straining, apologises, then tries again to grab it after it slides out of his reach as he breathes. I ask him if he will able to piss and he says he will manage, just to give him some time. We oblige and wait. He takes another 5 or so minutes to finally manage to hold the jar and piss enough urine into it to be accepted. He washes the jar then hands it to me and I label and bag it, him signing each step. We escort him to the door and another one is done.

We continue to process urine tests for the morning with little fanfare. All the prisoners except one are able to produce on demand. The one that can not produce, Stan Sutcliff, has three hours to produce and remains in the cell during muster. We ask him again once muster is correct and he refuses. He has an hour left and is happy to wait. We continue to process the ones called up and we get through another 8. Stan has just 5 minutes left when we ask him a final time and he is happy to give it another go. We walk him into the room and do the strip. Once done he turns to the toilet with his pants around his ankles, desperately trying to piss. He stands there for a good two minutes, his face getting redder and redder.

"I'm trying, Boss." he cries, the strain visible on his face.

"Last chance, Stan. You've had 3 hours man." I say and he gives an almighty groan as his teeth clench, his face grimaces and he turns almost purple. He farts, jerks forward and a turd comes shooting out of his arse, hitting the floor sideways. The officer in the booth begins to bellow and Tony starts gagging. Stan begins to apologise profusely, bends and scoops it up in his bare hands. I throw him some toilet paper and squeeze my nose shut. He wipes the floor and deposits the turd into the toilet, flushing it away. The only thought that comes to my mind is that I don't get paid enough for this.

The rest of the day is nothing compared to finding straws jammed down the eye of a dick, fat guys who can't reach their dicks and being fired upon with turd projectiles. The Sup drops by a couple of hours later and notifies the crook that he will be charged with interfering with a urinalysis test and returned to his unit. We end the day by completing 27 of the 30 assigned and are happy when the day is over. It really is a shitty day and I whistle as I drive out of the place.

Saturday, July 14, 2018

Rostered Day off

Sunday, July 15, 2018

Rostered Day Off

Monday, July 16, 2018

Rostered Day Off

Tuesday, July 17, 2018

Today I was rostered in Campaspe. Not a very exciting shift and more frustration than anything else. For one, being a main stream unit, you are stuck in the officer's station for pretty much the entire shift. It begins to get really monotonous after an hour or so and by lunchtime you are ready to put on a white jacket. Backwards. I am rostered with Vanessa Green and Russel Rawsley and am grateful that I have someone to chat to at least. We begin with morning muster and its called correct a short time later. I begin to unlock the cells as Vanessa begins to get things ready for the moves around the prison. Being a main stream unit, prisoners don't need to be escorted but are allowed to move around themselves as long as they are in possession of their ID card. The ID card has a bar code and some of the gates have readers on them making their move less of a hassle. They can get to far more places alone. That makes it easier on officers, but unfortunately it also means we don't get to leave the unit for escorts. For me personally, I prefer protection so you can at least leave the unit occasionally to go and escort a crook.

Once the cells are unlocked, there is a rush for the toasters with a couple of prisoners forced to make toast for a few, especially those that are standing over them. Stand-overs are a common thing and unfortunately challenging to eliminate. A line quickly forms at the toasters as the morning medication trolley enters the unit. I crack a smile as I see some prisoners begin looking from the toaster to the nurse and vice versa. Hmmm, what to choose. Vanessa calls for morning medication and a line forms just as quickly at the dispensing window, ID's in hand. Russel offers to stand and check and I check my emails. Nothing really exciting to see and I delete just as fast as I read. The only one that catches my eye is the one that tells me my annual leave has been approved for the 28th. I can not wait. A couple of prisoners fire up at the nurse but that is nothing new and Russel manages to calm them down quite quickly, assisted by other prisoners who want to get their own medication.

Once the medication trolley leaves, a number of prisoners approach the station for permission to go to the gym, a popular activity. Each unit is allocated a specific time slot and this morning it's Campaspe. We OK 22 to go and they leave, Vanessa writing them out in the book accordingly. The phone rings and its the laundry. They are ready for their workers and we call them up to the station. The prison has a number of areas that prisoners work in, earning themselves around ten bucks a day in wages. There is the wood shop, metal shop, laundry, kitchen and maintenance. Some of the areas are designated to main stream while others are for protection. The wood shop calls next and the dozen or so also leave. With quite a few prisoners returning to their cells and the number that went to the gym and work, the unit is eerily quiet. Just the low groan of TV's, radios and the occasional cough. Russel and I decide that it's probably a good time to conduct our random cell searching and we look at the list and head for the first cell.

It's a workers cell which makes it easy as he is not around to fire up. We enter the cell and begin to have a look around. We check the obvious places where contraband can be hidden like down the drain, in the mattress, in between clothing, in socks or shoes, food containers, places like that. Once done, we begin looking in areas that aren't as obvious like the screw mechanism in the fan, rolled into toilet paper rolls and sewn into the shower curtain. Prisoners have a lot of time on their hands to do nothing but think and sometimes they find ingenious ways to find new ways to hide contraband.

The cell checks out clean and we head to our next one, another worker. We smell the faint odour or cigarette smell as soon as we enter. Cigarettes are contraband with the banning a few years ago and prisoners have found great ways to simulate them. One of the most common is to stand over new prisoners for their nicotine patches, something they can request for up to ten weeks when first entering the prison system. They then take a few tea bags and boil them together with the nicotine patch. They run the tea through a tea towel, successfully straining the leaves and compress them in between layers of paper and or tea towels until dry. Then they roll the tea leaves into the good old bible pages and there you have it. Teabacco cigarettes. It doesn't take us long to locate the teabacco, hidden between the kettle and the kettle base. We confiscate it and continue searching, although nothing else is found.

Our third cell is for Nathan Turner and he is lying on his bunk watching TV as we enter. He doesn't appear concerned about our search and once we finish the strip search, he leaves and we begin. It's a very neat cell and Nathan has a few books and magazines stacked on his shelves. Books and magazines can be good hiding spots when officers cant be bothered conducting a thorough check. Magazines can be popular, especially for porn. A prisoner will rip out pages from a porn magazine and then insert the pages into another type of mag, such as a car mag. Then when they come in through admissions, they may have a stack of a dozen or so mags and the officer simply grabs the bundle and puts them in the cell bag, effectively handing the unit a fistful of porn. Porn, of course, is contraband. I take a look and they all check out. After a few more minutes of poking around, we exit the cell and head back to the station. The teabacco is bagged in an evidence satchel and sealed, signed and a report is typed up ready for the Sup who shows up half an hour later. It's Clare and Russel hands her our find. She thanks us and goes and does her Sup things. We go back to doing our boredom.

Lunchtime count comes just as the gym crooks return to the unit, and once correct, the kitchen workers dish out lunch. They ask us if we want some but none of us do. The afternoon consists of workers returning and other workers going for their afternoon shifts, medical runs, a couple of social workers making their daily rounds as well as watching crooks play pool, table tennis, boxing bag and using the fitness equipment in the unit, like the bike and treadmill. It really is a tough life for a prisoner. There is the daily religious rounds by all the appropriate representatives even including a Monk. Everyone is catered for.

Evening lock up count comes and pretty soon we are locking the cells, closing the chapter on yet another day. There were no codes, no fights, no arguments, no disagreements and no events. It was just a plain, run of the mill day in Campaspe.

Today was a good day.

Wednesday, July 18, 2018

Today I was rostered in Admissions again. As I walked into the unit, Raj met me and I learn that he has been offered a permanent gig in here. I congratulate him and put my things away. He tells me that the list for today is quite decent and when I see it, know what he means. There are 32 courts, 28 outgoing transfers and 24 incoming transfers. I put on some gloves and join the crew already processing the courts. Raj is stripping so I offer to spot for him. He is becoming a lot more confident, even able to tell some jokes along the way. As we finish stripping each prisoner, I point them towards the next officer that walks them to their allocated cell to wait for their ride. It becomes almost a production line with some officers standing at the counter handing out clothes, others stripping and spotting, some walking crooks to their cells and others out loading buses as they show up. A couple of prisoners fire up slightly at not being allowed to take books on the bus but rules are rules and they are stowed in their property box.

It takes a good hour and a half to process all the courts, but all eventually leave on their bus, leaving admissions nice and quiet as morning count is called. A short time later there is a recount called and we quickly do a walk around to ensure we truly are empty. We are empty and breathe a sigh of relief. The fault is elsewhere. The problem with a late morning count and unlock is that the prisoners require 12 hours of unlock per day. A late unlock means a late lock up and the longer it takes, the longer the units remain unlocked. This doesn't affect us here though, as we have set times to work and no lock ups to worry about. A few minutes later count is called correct and we await the arrival of our outgoing transfers.

Its 10 minutes later and the first of the transfers begin to roll in. Some with a little property and some with a lot. It's funny how prison works. A beefy guy shows up and he carries 2 or 3 bags of property. A small and wiry guy turns up and he carries half a bag. It's when a small guy turns up wheeling a tub full of bags that you begin to question the norm. You know that it's either that he is a really friendly kind of guy, or he has the ability to provide either sexual favours or drug related favours. And you can normally tell which. I try not to get involved in that side though as I am here to strip, and strip is what I do. Raj and I swap roles and it's my turn to live some nakedness. I begin to strip them then Raj walks them to their cells. The process repeats many times over, one prisoner leading to the next and so on. It becomes a repeating highlights reel of naked dicks and butts as I strip one then another and another. Nothing found, nothing said, nothing noted. Just one after the other. Half way through, Raj and I again swap and he takes the helm.

It goes on like that for the better part of the morning until we finally process the last one. Once I close the cell, I sit and take a break with the rest of the crew, enjoying my first cup of coffee since the last one at home. It's 11.30 and the crooks are already banging up, asking where the buses are. Again we shut them up with food, the sandwiches fulfilling their double duties. Lunchtime count is called shortly after and we do the rounds in pairs, Raj and I teaming up, him dropping traps and me writing the numbers. Once we have finished, I take the number, 28, to the person on the book and they call it in to control once they have confirmed the number with a couple of other teams. We talk shit as we await count correct. 10 minutes later count is called incorrect and we repeat the process, changing team members. I pair up with Gary Dales, a regular in here. Raj teams up with an officer from the last course, Jude Trevally. I drop the traps and Gary takes the numbers down. Once we complete our second circuit, he confirms the number as 28. Again that sigh of relief. The book calls it in shortly after and we sit around once more, talking shit again. 10 minutes later and count is called incorrect once more.

When a count is called incorrect a second time, units are required to swap with nearby units to ensure they aren't making the same mistake. We all head outside and swap with Tambo West, and their staff go and conduct the admissions count. Gary and I decide to stay as a team and do the rounds. When finished we ensure everyone has the same number, 51, and I call it in to control. We patiently wait in silence and let out a unified groan as count is called incorrect again.

"For fuck sake." Gary said, frustrated.

"How hard is it to count heads." I said. We repeat the process a second time then call in the same number, 51. Count has now been going for over 45 minutes and I could just imagine the line of buses sitting outside the jail. We sit around some more, literally twiddling our thumbs and when count is called incorrect again, almost throw our radios at the wall. With 4 counts now incorrect, we return to our respective units and conduct an ID in hand muster. Every prisoner is identified individually with the muster and their ID. We head back into admissions and are told that the count is one under. That means someone is missing and could mean an escape of some sort. With this many recounts, managers and higher are all involved as an escape could mean severe repercussions. We conduct our recount and given the complexity, it takes a good 40 minutes to finish. It is now close to two hours late. Some of the crooks voice their frustration as we conduct the count and we tell them there is nothing we can do. They have to grin and bear it just like us.

Just as we are about to count the last cell, I hear a string of profanity from the far end of admissions.

"What the fuck are you doing in here? Who put you in there?" We all walk over and see a small Asian prisoner, maybe 25 years old. He is pointing at his mouth and shaking his head. He doesn't speak English. He had been locked in a small toilet, situated in one of the far corners of the admissions area. The prisoner looked around and pointed at Jude Trevally. The person who unlocked him is a manager, Shane Thompson.

"Did you put him in there?" Shane asks of Jude. Jude is the shade of scarlet and looking very nervous.

"He needed to go to the toilet and all the cells were full." he said defensively.

"So you shove him into a staff toilet for one, then leave him in there and then forget about him completely. Is that right?" Shane said, clearly pissed off. "THIS COUNT HAS BEEN GOING

FOR OVER 2 FUCKING HOURS!" he yells. Jude just looks at the floor and remains quiet. Shane takes his radio and calls it in to control. A second later count is called correct. People disperse and head off to other areas, leaving Jude to himself. A golden rule when new is ASK. If you are unsure of what to do then ask someone. Jude will no doubt receive a written warning for this little fuck up, but at least he will learn from it.

The buses begin rolling up almost immediately and all the drivers begin questioning the delay. There is a lot of chatter, laughter, whispers and pointing as the story is relayed. Jude takes it on the chin and even joins in some of the banter. After all, it was a simple fuck up and it has been corrected. Given that it was the middle of the day, it didn't interrupt everyone's day too much. If it had of been at the end of the shift at lock up, then that would have been a disaster.

The prisoners are all loaded an hour or so later and a number of court returns are processed along the way. There are still a few courts to return and they will keep us busy throughout the afternoon. The good thing is, that day's midday muster is the only excitement to report to you. The rest of the day went smooth and involved nothing more than more stripping, more processing and more counts. Nothing that you haven't heard before and nothing that you will miss out on not reading about.

Today was an interesting day.

Thursday, July 19, 2018

Today I was rostered in Loddon North, a protection unit and mostly filled with prisoners who have been in the system for a long time. Not a lot of changes occur in there and the unit tends to run quite smoothly because of it. Incoming transfers have been known to upset the apple cart at times and not having them means things remain the same. The prisoners in the unit are mostly rated as sex predators, mostly charged with sex crimes involving rape, incest and paedophilia. I find it easiest to work in these units when I don't know the charges for individual prisoners. There are of course the high profile ones that everyone recognises and those you deal with as they come up but for the most part, I don't know them and I don't know what they are in for specifically.

I am joined in the unit by two other officers, Rob Delaney, an officer from my intake course and Rachel Ward. They are both normal officers in this unit and it will make the day that much easier. We meet and greet and have a quick catch up before morning count is called which Rachel and I undertake. I grab the muster and Rachel opens the traps. We start on the bottom tier and tick off the names, then head upstairs. We are about half way through when Rachel opens a trap to cell 32. The name on the door reads Smith and it doesn't mean anything to me. Rachel tells me one, as in one prisoner and is about to close it again when I hear a soft voice come through.
"Scuse me, Miss.?" She stops and peers back in. It is quite dark in the cell and she can make out the prisoner standing towards the back of the cell.
"What's up, Greg?" she asks.
"Can you please take this?" he says and steps forward, placing something on the trap. Rachel peers at it, then takes a step back. I look at it and at first am unsure of what it is. At first I thought it was a sausage, maybe left over from the previous night's dinner. Then my stomach turns as I come to shocking realisation what it is. It turns out to be his dick. Rachel has already got her radio to her mouth and calls an urgent code mike. I turn the lights on and see the prisoner with a large patch of blood on his pants. The

penis doesn't have a clean cut and by the serrations visible, can only imagine the horror that he must have felt when removing it. He is ghostly pale and sits on his bed.

"Medical are on the way, mate." I say through the trap and we wait for the nurses to show up. We keep Greg talking and when the Sup comes in, we get the OK to crack the cell.

He had used a plastic knife to hack his penis off. The nurses begin working on him, stopping the flow of blood and the whole time he kept talking to himself.

"I don't want it anymore. I don't want it anymore." He clearly had mental issues and needed more than just medical help. The nurses do an amazing job and not only calm him down but stop the blood and get him talking about something else. A stretcher turns up and the prisoner is lifted onto it and taken out of the unit. His cell his locked and we continue with our count, now minus 1. Once we finish our count and call it in, Rachel and I begin writing our report for the Sup regarding the morning amputation. Count is called correct and Rob heads out of the station to unlock the unit. There is a rush of feet toward the toasters and a number of prisoners turn toward us, anxious to find out what happened. Most can hear and see quite well from their cells so already know most of it anyway, but for those that don't are quickly filled in by their fellow room mates.

The morning medical trolley arrives and this is one of the units where practically every single prisoner has medication. They all begin to line up and I go to supervise the operation. The one thing that always gets me in these types of units is the politeness from the prisoners. 99% of them are so well mannered that you actually appreciate working in here. That is until you remind yourself of what they are in for. The manners are probably due to the fact that if they were ever exposed to a mainstream prisoner, they would suffer some pretty severe retribution. We are the only thing standing between them and that pain.

The nurse begins to dispense the medication and I begin to check the open mouths as they are presented to me. No one argues, no one attempts to divert and no one jumps the queue. Before I know it, everyone is dosed and back to their regular activities. A fourth officer comes into the unit and it's Raj. I greet him and he tells me he is working OT today. His first OT shift since he started and I congratulate him, a little jealous. It's always better to be working for double pay. He is here to escort a prisoner to medical and Rachel calls him up. Raj takes him and I have a read of my emails. It doesn't take me long and turn the computer off. Rob begins telling me about his upcoming holiday to Greece. I am jealous for the second time that day, a destination I have always wanted to visit. I tell him how much I love Greek history and he agrees with me. He has all the main places already on his itinerary, especially Santorini, Mykonos and Athens. I am happy for him and he shares his excitement as it is his first ever overseas holiday. Rachel agrees and also shares her passion for overseas travel. I have never been for an overseas holiday myself and understand how excited he must be.

Lunchtime muster goes off without a hitch, count called correct shortly after. There is a code Foxtrot called in one of the machine shops and a code mike called shortly after. That's normally how Foxtrots go. First they have some sort of fisty-cuffs then one needs the doctor. Most of them are over before anyone can react anyway. Punch here, punch there, punch back and boom, finished. They sort it out quickly and efficiently. The afternoon med trolley arrives soon after and I again head down to give them a hand and again it all runs smoothly. Lots of thank yous, pleases and have a great days are exchanged, but no fuck yous, jam 'em nor I wants. Everyone is handed their meds, everyone swallows them and everyone returns to their activities. Now why can't every unit be like this.

The afternoon is fairly quiet. I start to think that maybe, apart from that morning's events, we might have a perfect day. That is until we get a phone call from admissions. There is a new prisoner ready for pick up and Raj is already there ready to get him when we are ready. He was a late add on and not on the original daily list. Rachel scans the muster and allocates him to a cell on the top tier. With 3 free cells in the unit, no one is required to share. It's a good thing and keeps everyone happy. We call Raj on the radio and confirm his move. He acknowledges and begins the transfer.

The prisoner's name is Gus Van Fankel. He and Raj enter the unit and judging by his body language, he was going to be trouble. He marches straight up to the desk and fronts Rachel.

"I need a single cell." he demands instantly. Rachel just stands there, staring at him. They have a bit of a stare of and he repeats himself.

"I need a single-"

"I heard you. You don't run this unit, I do. I conduct the interview." she says calmly. His face grows red and he looks a little flustered.

"Sorry, Miss. I need a single cell. I've been here before." he repeats a third time, but Rachel holds her own.

"And again, I heard you. I will conduct the induction interview and you will find out all the information you need." she says, still calm.

"But I'm just saying, I-"

"And I need you to shut your mouth." she says, cutting him off and he closes his lips, clearly not happy. He is a small wiry looking man of about 50, with round, thin wired glasses on the end of his nose and a very diminished head of hair. Rachel then proceeds to conduct the interview, telling him all about the unit rules, policies, some day to day requirements and finally his cell allocation.

"I need a cell on the bottom tier." he snaps at her, cutting her off. She takes a step back and just looks at him. Then at me and back at him.

"I have given you your cell allocation. I suggest you go to it."

"I need a bottom tier cell. I have bad knees and can't climb stairs." he starts but Rachel has switched off, closing his file and sitting at the computer.

"I suggest you go, mate." I say. A cardinal rule with officers is to always back your colleague. Whether you agree or not, always back them. Van Fankel looks at her a final time, then picks his bag up and heads for his cell. Rachel turns to me and gives me that WTF look. I know exactly what she's thinking.

I decide to have a wander around the unit and begin taking a walk. I stick my head in to a couple of cells and do some welfare checks, ensuring all is OK. I then head upstairs and do the same. As I pass Van Fankel's cell, he sticks his head out.
"Excuse me, Boss." I turn to him.
"Yes?"
"I really need a cell on the bottom tier." he says.
"Do you have a certificate?" I ask and he shakes his head.
"Never needed one before."
"Unfortunately there are no cells available on the bottom and if you need one then you need a certificate. If you had one then you may be moved to a unit with one available." I inform him but he doesn't like my answer.
"But I have really bad-"
"You don't like listening, do you?" I ask him.
"Fine. I'll go on a hunger strike then." he says folding his arms.
"You do that. But unless you make an appointment to see the doctor, then there is nothing anyone can do." I say and continue my walk. He slams the cell door closed and the bang reverberates around the unit. I look at the station and Rachel looks at me and rolls her eyes. Rob just shakes his head. I finish my walk and head back to the station, taking a seat and accepting the coffee Rob hands me.
"What a fuckwit." he adds. I agree with him and sip. We spend the rest of the afternoon relaxing, not much activity happening until the afternoon medication trolley turns up. Everyone lines up except our new arrival, his door staying closed. Rob heads to the line and conducts mouth inspections, everyone presenting as per the previous rounds and it's all over quite quickly. Afternoon muster is called soon after and everyone stands by their doors. Rachel buzzes Van Fankel on the intercom but all she can hear is a muffled grunt. She asks him again to stand by his open door and the response is more aggravated, still muffled grunting. I take the muster sheet and begin walking cell to cell. When I reach Van Fankel's closed door, I tap it but it doesn't open. I take out my key

and override his internal lock. I open the door and see him standing in the middle of his cell, arms by his side, just looking at me.

"You coming out?" I ask him and he grunts.

"Is that a yes?" and he grunts louder. He takes a step towards me and when I see the issue I nearly drop the muster sheet. I can not stop the smile that lands on my face, a small chuckle escaping as I try and speak.

"Would you...like me to-" but I can't continue, the laugh getting caught in my throat. Rob and Rachel are looking up from below and can not see what I can see. I wave them up, hanging on to the hand rail. Rob reaches the cell first and immediately turns back when he sees. Rachel doesn't.

"I suppose you think that's gonna help you in some way." she says, pissed off. He grunts again, more aggravated. She pulls out her radio and for the second time that day, calls a code mike. Gus Van Fankel has sewn his lips shut.

Now at least we knew why he couldn't answer us over the intercom. He had done a pretty good job and the stitches looked neat and in line, almost OCD level. The unit becomes a buzz as he exits his cell and hangs on to rail, other prisoners cackling, hooting and cheering. Gus's face remains stony, his demeanour never changing. The Sup, Clare, enters the unit and one look tells her all she needs to know. The medical team arrive and OK the Tac boys to escort the prisoner to the medical unit under his own steam and he walks out with his escort, giving Rachel one final glare.

We finish count and it is called correct almost as soon as we call it in, control obviously waiting for us. The evening goes smoothly and uneventful. We receive a phone call from Clare ab out an hour later to say that Gus was coming back. The doctor refused his request for a medical and apparently he tried to say he felt in danger as Rachel and I had bullied him on his arrival. Clare refused his request and said he would be returning to his allocated cell. He entered the unit a short time later and didn't peep a word. He didn't even look in our direction.

Final lock up came and went and we all walked out together, still laughing, almost in stitches about..the stitches.

Friday, July 20, 2018

Rostered Day Off

Saturday, July 21, 2018

Rostered Day Off

Sunday, July 22, 2018

Rostered Day Off

Monday, July 23, 2018

Today I was sick and have taken a couple of days off. It's a cold and the headache is what gifts me with a medical certificate for two days. The mental image of a penis sitting on the trap is also still playing on my mind and I try hard to block it out. I'm not sure what would prompt someone to slice off their own appendage, but with a plastic knife??

Tuesday, July 24, 2018

Today is my second sick day. I still feel pretty shitty and decide not to put myself down for overtime.

Wednesday, July 25, 2018

Rostered Day Off

Thursday, July 26, 2018

Rostered Day off

Friday, July 27, 2018

Today I was rostered back in Loddon North. I am more than a little excited to see how Gus ended up. He seemed so intent on trying to manipulate the system, I'm more than interested to see if he succeeded. As I enter the unit, I see Rachel already at the officer's station and she gives me a thumbs up as she sees me. I point up to Gus's cell, she looks up over her shoulder and makes a growling face. She points at a cell in the bottom corner and I realise he must have gotten his way, somehow.
"How?" I ask as soon as I am in the station.
"Tony Malone." she says.
"What? How? He isn't normally in here?"
"He was in here with 2 blow ins and didn't bother running it past the Sup first. That guy really pisses me off." she replies and I can see it written all over her face. Looks like Gus managed to get his own way while no one was looking. It happens quite a bit unfortunately, especially when no regular staff are working in the unit. Crooks take advantage and you can't really blame them. It is their job after all.

Our third officer comes in shortly after, Jacob Davidson.
"Hi Jacob." I say as he approaches and we shake hands. He is a good officer and always happy to help. He shakes Rachel's hand and goes to put his bag away.
"How has the unit been?" I ask.
"Pretty good. Quiet as usual." she says and I know what she means. I hope that is the case today as I feel a headache coming on.

We start to conduct trap to trap muster, me with the sheet and Rachel dropping traps. We get to cell 8 and she peers in, the name on the door is Van Fankel. I can feel the expression on his face through the trap and Rachel doesn't say a word. We continue our count and once finished, I call in the number once called for by Control. It's called correct a few minutes later and I do the rounds unlocking the cells. The prisoners all begin to exit their cells and most head for the toasters, a couple to the phones and one to the laundry. The morning medication trolley arrives and Rachel heads off to assist them, while I check my emails. Nothing noteworthy except one. It's from one of the administration staff. They are writing to me to ask whether I would accept a permanent role in Loddon North. I am instantly torn. I love the unit, the simplicity of it. It's known as one of the retirement units amongst the other officers and know it's a good place to hang my hat. But the other side of my heart is telling me not to. And the reason being what you are reading right now. I know that if I was to work in a unit, I would not have nearly enough material to be able to fill a month worth of excitement for you to read. Especially in a unit as quiet as Loddon North. Admissions maybe, even Visits would be OK but not here. I think about it for a few minutes then write my response, a very polite no thank you. Unless of course you guys think I should. I've even opened an email address if you would like me to work in a unit full time. It's listed at the end of the book.

Anyway, I typed my response and pressed send without a second thought. As I close the email, there is a frantic call of a code Alpha in visits. I look at the clock and wonder if they would even have any prisoners up there yet. Turns out they did have one, a billet, in for the morning clean before the visitors show. Turns out he had helped himself to some of the staff's lunches and snacks and when confronted had taken a swing at the officer, Vanessa Green. She sustained a broken tooth and cut lip and he was in a world of pain about two seconds later when 3 large Tactical boys took him to ground. He is taken to Admissions and transported out of the prison about half an hour later. The process following an assault on an officer is always swift and final and always with the removal of the prisoner.

Subsequent phone calls to Visits inform us that Vanessa is fine, just shaken and off to see her dentist. She will most likely have a couple of days off for that punch and so she should.

Jacob, Rachel and I are sitting in the station drinking coffee when we hear a commotion coming from the far corner of the unit on the top tier. Two prisoners appear to be having some sort of disagreement and they are in each other's face. No punches are being thrown but a lot of finger pointing and that can be a good indication that things are about to get physical. We all get up and Jacob and I head over to see what the problem is. Rachel remains in the station as one officer is required to man the station permanently. We head up stairs and try and calm the boys down. They seemed to be arguing over the mop and bucket.

"It's fucken my turn. I been waiting." one cried.

"I got it first, mate. Shoulda been quicker ya dickhead." the yells back.

"Guys, guys, guys." Jacob yells at them. "It s a mop and bucket. Geez."

"But boss, I been wai-". But he is cut off.

There is a scream of pain from the other side of the unit. We look just in time to see Van Fankel drop a bucket and run back to his cell. Rachel is screaming from the officers station, pulling her jumper off. The bastard had thrown a bucket of hot water on her. He used the altercation to his advantage and wasted no time in using his freshly boiled kettle while we were here and she was there alone. I call a code Alpha and request urgent medical help for an officer. I run to close Gus in the cell and Jacob runs to Rachel. He grabs a blanket and holds it over her as she begins ripping some of her clothing off. People don't realise that when someone is hit with hot water, the hot water can get soaked into clothing and continue burning. She lays down on the floor crying, her pain clearly audible. The doors burst open a flood of officers come running in including the nurses. They run to the station and begin treating Rachel, officers helping move her on to a stretcher. The Sup heads for the cell holding Gus and cracks the trap, whispering something I don't hear. I know what the nest step is for Gus and Tactical boys are already gearing up to enter the cell. "He is just sitting there, boys." the Sup says to them and they peer in. They crack the cell and head in, three squeezing into the small room. We hear a cry of pain as they handcuff him and drag him out. The same stony look is on his face and no sign of remorse. They drag him out of the unit, his eyes never leaving the floor. I

don't know whether that was his intention or whether he just
wanted to hurt Rachel. Sometimes prisoners are known to assault
staff as a way of bailing out of a unit when there is no other way
out. I decide I don't care what his intention was, I'm just glad he is
gone. Whatever his sentence was, he can now add an assaulting
an officer charge which can carry up to ten additional years. I
know that with our justice system, he will never get ten years but
I hope he gets the most possible anyway.

Rachel is wheeled out of the unit a short time later, her face
covered in some sort of gauze. I gently touch her shoulder as she
wheels past me and she looks at me, her eyes doing the talking for
her. The Sup stands the code down and Jacob and I begin to write
our reports. We finish almost at the same time and just sit there in
silence for a bit. The unit has taken on that all too familiar silence
and we wait for another officer to replace Rachel who would be
on her way to hospital now. Raj walks in a short time later and we
fill him in on what's happened. He looks shocked and voices his
anger.

That was how the morning came to a close for us. It's truly sad to
see officers, both male and female, assaulted, spat on, have shit
and piss thrown on them, be abused and just be spoken to like
shit, just because they work as a correctional officer.
Unfortunately prisoners believe they have a right to treat staff as
they do. But every case of assault is passed on to police and fully
investigated. In most cases, prisoners are charged and time added
to their sentence.

The afternoon was the exact opposite to the morning. Everything
ran smooth and efficiently. The med runs all went without the
slightest hiccup and musters were done in almost complete
silence. When we lock the prisoners in their cells during the final
lock down, a couple of them ask about Rachel and ask us to pass
on their well wishes. They are as shocked as we are and know that
these sort of units always run smoother when regular staff man
them. Having one of the regular staff off injured only means a
blow in comes to replace them and that can upset the apple cart.

Jacob and I walk out together when count is called correct. He says he'll give the hospital a call and check on Rachel and will let me know. I thank him. And I thank him for his help today. And as I walk through the outside gate and into the car park, I remember one important thought that was told to me by an officer long ago.

Any day that you get to walk out of a maximum security prison at the end of the shift, is a good day.

Today was definitely NOT a good day.

Saturday, July 28, 2018

Annual Leave (Yay!!)

Sunday, July 29, 2018

Annual Leave

Monday, July 30, 2018

Annual Leave

Tuesday, July 31, 2018

Annual Leave

Final Note

I would like to thank you personally, for allowing me to share with you some genuine experiences that occurred in our prison this month. Like last month, the events that happened have shaped some officer's lives, some prisoner's lives and ultimately shown just how volatile and crazy things can get. The descriptions do no justice compared to actually being involved in these incidents and I highly recommend trying out for a role within a correctional facility if you find these books interesting.

Prison Days August Edition is already available for Pre-Order.

Thank you for your continued support.

Simon King

prisondays@yahoo.com

I have tried to recreate events, locales and conversations from my memories of them. In order to maintain their anonymity in some instances I have changed the names of individuals and places, I may have changed some identifying characteristics and details such as physical properties, occupations and places of residence.

Printed in Great Britain
by Amazon

22569957R00037